Real Estate Investing
Hints Tips and Strategies

By: Kaye Dennan
ISBN-13: 978-1492234029

Real Estate Investing

TABLE OF CONTENTS

Publishers Notes

Dedication

Chapter 1- Introduction

Chapter 2- Ways To Make Money With Property Investing

Chapter 3- Buying Entities

Chapter 4- Going To Contract

Chapter 5- Buying Strategies

Chapter 6- Setting Your Buying Criteria

Chapter 7- Strategies For Absorbing Interest Rate Increases

Chapter 8- Turning Negatively Geared Real Estate Into Positive Cash Flow Real Estate

Chapter 9- Finance

Chapter 10- Property Management

Chapter 11- Business Plan

Chapter 12- Building Your Team Of Experts

Chapter 13- Selling Your Investment Real Estate

Check List For Purchasing Investment Property

About The Author

Kaye Dennan

PUBLISHERS NOTES

Disclaimer

This publication is intended to provide helpful and informative material. The information, advice and strategies contained herein may not be suitable for your situation.

You should consult with a professional where appropriate.

The author shall not be liable for any loss of profits or any other commercial damages, including but not limited to special, incidental, consequential, or other damages. The author and publisher specifically disclaim all responsibility for any liability, loss or risk, personal or otherwise, which is incurred as a consequence, directly or indirectly, from the use or application of any contents of this book.

Any and all product names referenced within this book are the trademarks of their respective owners. None of these owners have sponsored, authorized, endorsed, or approved this book.

© Copyright Kaye Dennan 2013
Paperback Edition
Manufactured in the United States of America

DEDICATION

To Mandy and Peter who work so hard to build a lifestyle free from monetary worries for themselves and their children, Riley, Jai and Ellie.

Kaye Dennan

INTRODUCTION

Building wealth through real estate investing is an age old strategy for securing your financial future. It has been happening since time began and will continue to happen long after we have left this earth.

There is no more ground to acquire and in fact it is being eroded away one way or another. This fact alone and of course, along with population growth, ensures that the value of the necessities of life will continue to grow in value. Oil, gold, timber, steel and food of all sorts are just other examples of how the demands force the cost of items up if the items are in short or limited supply.

No matter what country you live in, you would have either experienced a housing equity drop in real estate or you would have seen it happening somewhere near you. Some countries are recovering faster from the GFC effect than others and some countries like Australia did not actually suffer too severely during these last two years.

Again, back to where you live….You are probably now seeing different areas where real estate prices are starting to level out or in fact starting to increase in price as people feel more confident about their financial future.

In this ebook, **'Real Estate Investing Hints, Tips & Strategies'** our aim is to help guide you in understanding how to build a property investment portfolio. There are many steps to be taken when building a property portfolio and there are many steps to avoid.

The aim of **'Real Estate Investing Hints, Tips & Strategies'** is to walk you through the purchasing process and make you aware of some of the pitfalls that a beginner property investor (someone with less than 3 properties) may experience. You will need to confirm your thoughts and research with your advisers as to the facts discussed so that you act in your best interest for the area in which you live or in which you intend to purchase. Do keep in mind that different countries and even different states in the same country may have a different set of rules for property investment especially regards property management and taxes.

Another aim is to give you alternatives to think about with property investing as there are so many different strategies that can be employed to grow your wealth. You may find that during one cycle of your property portfolio growth you will employ one strategy and during another when you have more time, you may employ another. Each and every investor has to set their own goals according to their own experience, finance abilities, time involvement and knowledge.

Property investing is no different than any other money making venture you may take on. It needs money, a well defined plan, a team of experts to work with, knowledge, the ability to make decisions and ACTION. (That may sound weird to you, but some people cannot make decisions and therefore look at hundreds of properties and are always saying "I missed out on that one", purely and simply because they could not bring themselves to put pen to paper. Fear took control.) This comes down to the psychological part of building a property investment portfolio, a very important part of the whole process.

We will take you through a Business Plan and give you points to consider so that you can make your decisions about your strategies. Keep in mind here that a Business Plan is a guide and can be changed at any time, according to changes of mind and changes in circumstances. Borrowing money for housing or property investing has become a lot harder and if you have a Property Investment Business Plan then you will be perceived by lenders as someone who has got their head around the industry and that you have worked through different options and know exactly where you are going. This will be a big plus when asking for a loan.

We will discuss what to look for when purchasing and property management will also be looked at as this is an area that does confuse some buyers. Finance will be talked about in general so that you understand various lending options.

And to finish up is a chapter on selling real estate because that too is an important part of realizing your profits when selling a property.

I hope your property investing goes well for you and that you reach your goals and have the lifestyle that can be achieved from a serious commitment to building a property portfolio.

Kaye Dennan

Ways To Make Money With Property Investing

'Investing in Real Estate' is a broad based term.

There are several ways to make money when investing in real estate but it would have to be said that the majority of people tend to think of 'investing in real estate' as buying and then renting the property out, hence, making money from the rental and eventually, capital gains. This is the simple explanation that older generations would think of when investing in real estate, the 'buy and hold' strategy', but let's look at property investing in the broader sense.

Buying, remodeling, selling

I have started with this strategy because it is one that is a little controversial. There are investors who do not regard this as 'property investing' because in their eyes the property is not being 'purchased and rented'.

Personally I take the view that this is property investing because it is putting money into property with the view to making a profit.

I liken it to share trading where you have investors who buy and hold shares for several months, buy and hold for periods of a few days up to a few months, or those that day trade. They are all classified as share traders, but each has a different trading strategy.

This is the same way I view the buying, remodeling, selling strategy. Each to their own, I guess.

This is where a buyer buys a property and immediately puts in tenants, or even buys a property where there are existing tenants. The intention being to hold the property long term and gain from capital increases, then possibly buy again when there is sufficient equity to do so. This is a slower system of making money in the property market, but in saying that a lot of investors are holding down jobs and cannot always be free to be more active in the market place. If this is the case then buying and holding is at least getting them in the market and building their equity for when they can be more active.

Buying, renting and selling

Experienced property investors will often use this strategy which is looking for an excellent buy, renting it for 2 – 3 years and then sell it on with a profit. If they do not intend to renovate then the property needs to be in good order and it is the excellent buying price that will be the sole purpose for the purchase.

In this case the buyer would buy and sit out a few years waiting for the price to increase sufficiently to cover costs and make a nice profit.

Buying, remodeling and renting

In this case a purchaser looks for a property that can be upgraded without spending too much money but at the same time gain in value. This allows the investor to ask for a higher rent than would have been expected in the first instance.

Firstly, there is the refurbishing strategy where only a few thousand dollars are spent on a repaint, a kitchen facelift which could be new cupboard doors and new stove, a bathroom refit or spruce up and maybe some new flooring, all of which could most likely be done for under $5,000 on a tight budget. A very strong argument for this system of investing is that, using a hypothetical case, you get increased rent due to the upgrade of approximately another $25 - $40 per week which could turn your property into a positive cash flow situation after completion.

The second scenario is where a property is purchased with the intent of a bigger remodeling job which could mean a total kitchen refit, new bathroom refit, another bedroom added, a garage added, new windows, new window trimmings, flooring and/or a new outdoor entertainment area. Also, while this is being done the house would be modernized as well. This all means that you could possibly add another 20-50% or more to the rent, depending on what value you actually do to the property.

Both actions would increase the value of the property, but the second system much more so. In fact with the second action the aim would be to get an increase in property value of about 25 – 55% higher over and above the cost of the renovation. In other words, if you spent $40,000 on the renovation you could be looking to a minimum total property increase of $50,000-$60,000.

This system is not for everybody as it takes more knowledge, time and extra funds but is one which investors often look at once they become more experienced and have a few properties in positive cash flow.

What step the investor takes from here varies. They may decide to hold for 10 – 15 years or they may sell the property on over the next 3 - 5 years.

And more.......

There are more strategies to making money through property investing but as a beginner it pays to do lots of research, look at lots of properties and decide which strategy you would like to start with. At a later date you may change your ideas as many people do the more knowledgeable and skilled they become.

There are endless opportunities in the renovating area, but again this takes time and money.

Buying Entities

A buying entity is the actual owner of the property. A buying entity could be a single person, a joint ownership, a group of people, a company, a trust or a superannuation group.

Before going to contract it pays to have the buying entity sorted out because if it is entered incorrectly and then you want to change it before settlement you may be up for two lots of taxes. Alternatively you might be able to crash the first contract and sign a second contract under the correct buying entity but this would cost some money as well.

All these details need to be discussed in full with your accountant and your solicitor before having a contract drawn up. If you choose to go in with other individuals there does need to be a drawn up agreement so that allocation of duties is clarified, how the loan will be funded, how it will be paid, how the handling of one person needing to leave the investment is to be handled, how income will be dealt with, how expenses will be paid, how long the property is held for, and so on. There are a lot of decisions to be made when owning real estate investments and the handling of all these issues needs to be in writing so that you don't end up with a forced sale on your hands to split up the cash.

In fact, if you have decided to purchase it is a good idea to have all this sorted out before you even go looking then you are not caught with wanting to go to contract on a property and not having the correct legal matters sorted out and being disappointed with your lost opportunity. It can take several weeks to get the right paperwork completed if you are setting up a trust or a partnership for instance.

Getting it right to benefit from tax

Your accountant plays a role at this point in helping you work out the entity because there are tax issues to consider and you want to get them right.

Getting the spelling correct

When purchasing a property it is important to even get the spelling of the buying entity right, because whatever is written on the contract is the legal owner of the property. If, for example, John K. Brown purchased a property and the buying entity of the property was entered as John M. Brown it could be legally possible for a John M. Brown to claim ownership of the property, or if the spelling was entered as John K. Browne that too could risk ownership.

You can see that it is imperative to check the spelling on any property document that you are signing before you sign it. If it is wrong, make the change and initial the change.

That means contracts to purchase, loan documents, insurance documents and any other documents that you may sign relating to the property.

Even it does not mean problems with ownership it will most likely incur you in extra legal costs.

GOING TO CONTRACT

There are several important steps to be aware of when going to contract on a property. Often buyers are scared to go to contract because they feel that once they have signed the contract they are committed, and in actual fact that could be the case if conditional clauses are not inserted.

If the contract is not set up correctly then a buyer can end up being committed without realizing it, but there are ways and means around that so that you do have time to finalize your finance and other issues related to the purchase.

Clauses can be added to contracts which allow you the time to check out certain issues or have certain things, like your finance approved. These clauses are called 'conditions of the contract'.

Clauses of note:

1. Finance Clause - most contracts these days, regardless of country or state, have a finance clause as part of the contract and all you have to do is enter the date that the finance has to be approved by (usually 2-3 weeks after the signing of the contract). If not, put one in yourself.

2. Building Inspection – make sure that you have 2 weeks from the date of signing the contract to have the property inspected by a building inspector to ensure that the building falls within the council's building requirements and that the building, fences or retaining walls are not riddled with termites or other undesirables.

3. Occupation clause – if there are unsuitable tenants in the property you may put a clause in that the property must be handed over 'in vacant possession' which means the seller would have to make sure that the property is vacated before settlement. If this was the case and there were unsavory tenants in the property I would also put a clause in the contract about the property being in a 'clean and habitable state' at takeover. This will meant that if the tenants have left it in a shocking state, the seller will have to pay to have someone clean it or they will have to do it themselves.

4. Other clauses – if there are any other points of discussion between the seller and the buyer that need clarifying, put a clause in the contract and set a date by which the issue is to be solved.

Having these contract conditions sets a date to have the issued resolved and it stops the seller from being concerned that time will slip away and the buyer will make an extra effort to have the issued completed on time. Time extensions can be made if both parties agree, but the seller if under pressure from another buyer may not necessarily agree to the buyer does need to act and make sure the time lines are met.

Settlement date

Have a good hard think about the date that you wish the contract to settle. 28 days was pretty much the norm, but with finance often taking longer for approval now, settlement is more likely to be 6 weeks.

You may choose a longer or shorter settlement date because of any of the following factors:
- A settlement date could be made to suit the property being vacated by the existing tenants
- You may wish to do renovations as soon as taking over the property so you might look at a 3 months settlement to give you time to measure up for alterations and order materials
- You might have found a property earlier than expected and need the extra time to put a few things in place before settlement
- A later settlement date may suit the sellers and not really bother you too much as to when it is
- You might set a later date in a contract but all issues are solved earlier and it suits both parties to bring the settlement date forward.

Finance

A ploy that is often used by cash home buyers is to put a finance clause in the contract and this way they can use that clause to get out of the contract if they wish. The point is, even if you have the cash, you are buying an investment property and therefore would most likely not pay cash for an investment property because you want the tax benefits. I would suggest you use the finance clause anyway.

Make sure you allow sufficient time to get finance approval. In most cases you can get a finance date extension, but not always, especially if you have managed to get a property at a good price. Chances are there will be another buyer waiting to find out how you got on. Don't be pressured by the real estate agent into putting too earlier a date for finance. They often want to push things ahead so that they can get their commission (can't blame them really) but you need to take control of the dates.

Property Insurance

Check to see if you need to take out property insurance. Usually a buyer needs to insure the property once a contract is signed as the signing date is the actual date of the purchase of the property and therefore the new owner needs to cover it.

BUYING STRATEGIES

Negative Gearing

A negatively geared property is one where the income from the property does not cover the interest on the loan on the property. In other words it is in negative income. This means that the owner will need to put money into the account to pay for the difference in loan repayments and also find money from their own sources to pay for the overheads of managing the property.

Here are a few reasons why investors negative gear:

- To offset a high personal income and reduce tax (their job or business)
- To allow them to purchase a higher priced property, usually in a better real estate area, with the expectation that capital growth will be above average
- Although the property is negatively geared, with the write-backs for tax, it will still end up being a cash flow positive property
- They do not have sufficient deposit to put down on a property to make it positively geared but are still able to pay the shortfall on a negatively geared property

Many accountants do not like negative gearing but if you talk to experienced investors it does seem to work, but care needs to be taken that you do not over step the mark and borrow so much money that should anything negative happen in your personal life that you cannot meet the shortfall.

In the next chapter we discuss the possibilities of turning a negatively geared property into a positive cash flow property.

Positive Gearing

A positively geared property is where the income from the property is in excess of the monies needed to pay the interest on the loan. This type of property certainly makes it easier for property investors regarding payments, but also the excess in income can be put back into the property in capital improvements (tax deductible) or to pay off more of the equity.

Do be aware that positive income is a taxable income.

Finding the sellers

When buying investment properties it is important to look for motivated sellers.

Motivated sellers are those that 'have a reason to sell and sell quickly' or at least reasonably quickly, because they do not want the property sitting around.

A motivated seller could have any of the following reasons for selling:
- An estate sale
- A marriage/partnership break up
- Relocation to distant places – overseas or interstate
- A seller who needs money to float their business or expand their business
- An investor who is over committed
- A landlord who doesn't want to be a landlord any longer
- Financial problems of the owner, especially if they are not meeting mortgage commitments
- The property has been on the market for a while now and the owner has to sell quickly

Setting Your Buying Criteria

A strategy that will save you a lot of time and money when trying to find the right real estate investment is to make a short list early on in your investment property search. You might wonder how to do this when there are so many properties on the market but this is easier than it seems.

There are thousands of properties on the market so the very first step to take is to know how much money you can spend.

This is a critical step for two reasons:

1. you don't want to be getting confused with your pricing by looking at properties that you cannot afford
2. if you do not make a short list the whole process becomes overwhelming and you might find you want to walk away from building your property portfolio and your future wealth

In the early stages your ability to service the loans needs to be a fairly strong consideration.

In saying that, do make sure that you seek out all avenues, don't take 'no' for an answer or even a low dollar value offer, there are many places and ways of find finance so be sure that you talk to everyone. Once you have gone down the path of building up a list of financiers it will be a lot easier next time.

Tip: before approaching individual banks and lending institutions, find out how things work in your country. Make sure that your credit rating is acceptable.

One step that some people take is to make several applications for loans and decide on none of them. What they are unaware of is that when an application is made to a lending institution it is lodged with the credit reporting company. If you make too many applications you may be penalized and find it very difficult to get a loan at all. This is one of the main reasons why people use mortgage brokers. They can work through a broker without a formalized application and not have their credit rating affected.

9 Secrets to Creating

I suggest you have these details in your Property Investment Business Plan so that you can use it each and every time you look for a property. By using these steps you will be comparing 'apples with apples' and not 'apples with potatoes'

1. Know how much you have to spend
2. Detail your location criteria – bus route, school, shops, etc
3. List the property requirements – 3 bedrooms, 2 bathroom, 1 garage, etc
4. Preference for building materials – wood, brick, etc
5. List desired outdoor features
6. List any other features that you may think is a bonus or benefit – a cul de sac, pool, landscaped garden
7. Whether you are prepared to do any upgrade to the property and at what level you are prepared to upgrade – a quick paint or a remodeling of rooms
8. Age of property
9. Location – the same area that you live in or how far away you are prepared to buy

When you are comparing properties that have the same criteria as each other you can make better and quicker decisions and feel more confident that you have made the right decision.

It is always so easy to get side tracked when you get into the property listing sites and if you do not have your own strict criteria you will find that the enjoyment of searching for a property soon wanes.

When you have your shortlist, do some property inspections and then short list again for your final decision making.

Where to buy

When purchasing investment real estate, investors want to achieve some capital gain either in the short term or in the long term. Here are some positive factors that successful investors look for when purchasing real estate to gain capital gains and also to get good rental incomes:

- Near good transport routes – buses or train lines or good road access
- In the CBD because cities are becoming more and more popular for unit living and younger people like to live there and leave the city for the weekends
- Near good schools
- Near universities – good for group rentals or for setting a house up in such a way that there are large bedrooms each with study areas and communal living areas
- Near water – near the seaside, canals or rivers
- In areas that have large commercial ventures going on or planned in the near future
- In areas that have rapid growth due to natural growth, commercial ventures, desirable weather or immigration

All of these features attract good rentals and good property gains.

Make up a check list so that when you have a short list you can refer to your check list and see what is there and what is missing with each property when comparing them.

If you are very tight for money and cannot raise the funds to purchase a property at the price you would like, consider purchasing on the outer suburbs of a large city because as the city grows around the property that you have bought, the capital gains will be very good. Keep in mind the comments about transport if you are going to purchase in the outer areas of a city.

The important thing is to get started. Decide on your own areas of interest for property investing and go for it.

Strategies For Absorbing Interest Rate Increases

Over the next few years it is going to be crucial that strategies are designed to absorb rising interest rates. Interest rates have been exceptionally low and the only way they will go is up. This means that when buying a property consideration should be given as to how the increased interest rates will be absorbed, or at least how they can be paid. As sure as day follows night, interest rates will rise from their current levels.

Here are some suggestions to keeping ahead of interest rates:

- increase rents (but this can usually only be done to a certain extent and not always enough to absorb a full interest rate increase)
- upgrade the look of the property by doing a quick paint through and general tidy up for about $5,000 which in turn should return a higher rental increase
- remodel and increase the rent substantially

Any work done with the purpose of increasing rent needs to be carefully thought out because any rent increase needs to absorb the cost, plus more to cover the interest rate increase as well.

Changes that are most likely to increase the rent are:

- A repaint – clean look (one coat is probably sufficient unless there is damage)
- New flooring if the flooring is in poor condition

- New kitchen bench tops and cupboard doors – or even painted doors can do wonders
- New tap fittings
- New curtains – or window coverings
- Security screens instead of fly screens as personal safety is a huge issue these days

With more expensive remodeling these improvements are the most valuable as far as increased rent is concerned (as well as the ones mentioned above):

- An extra bedroom
- Extra garaging
- Family room/entertainment room
- Outdoor entertainment area
- Sustainable living features

As well as the features mentioned above, a revamp of the garden is always a good idea and to make it as low maintenance as possible but still attractive. Lots of green always looks good.

What also needs to be kept in mind is whether the work you do is tax deductible through depreciation or whether you can write the cost of in the current financial year of the spending. Check this with your accountant so that you get the best tax benefits.

Kaye Dennan

Turning Negatively Geared Real Estate Into Positive Cash Flow Real Estate

A negatively geared investment is where the interest on the loan is in excess of the income from the property.

Let's look at the possibilities of turning a negatively geared property into a positive cash flow property.

To turn a negatively geared property into a positive cash flow property you either have to reduce your management expenses (that includes all expenses) so that they are less than the income from the property, and this is not easy to do.

Or you can work on the property so that you can increase the income from the property and therefore make the income higher than the total expenses of the property. This is usually the more effective way, but not always possible.

The reason this may not be possible could be because you won't be able to increase the rent much due to the location of the property or your loan repayments are so high that you won't be able to cover the shortfall anyway.

Turning negatively geared real estate into positive cash flow real estate may be an investment strategy that you purposely set out to achieve through steps that you undertake in making the property more attractive to renters and thereby being able to get a higher rent through the steps that you take.

There are different strategies that you may choose to use and I have listed some scenarios below for you to consider.

Some investors set out to solely look for real estate to improve before renting out, thereby getting a higher rental right from the first day of renting. Others will work on the properties they already have to gain extra income and/or capital from them.

Your involvement will depend on the amount of time you have available to be hands on with the job.   Usually those people who do major renovations are full-time investors or renovators.

Make a checklist for renovations.... list every single item to be changed so that you cost it exactly.

To Do A Radical Change Or Just An Upgrade

This decision often comes down to dollars and cents. If there is the money for grand remodeling and you are sure it will pay off, this could be the answer. Otherwise you may just look at a facelift.

Just giving your property a facelift of a few thousand dollars could mean that you can increase your rent by about $20-30 per week. This may be enough to give you positively cash flow.

A facelift like this would be using some elbow grease in the garden to make it a low maintenance garden with edging and few bush gardens. As well as this you would probably give the property a coat of paint throughout and new flooring in the kitchen. In a property that does need a spruce up, $4-5000 can often modernize it with some curtains and a few other extras that make the property more appealing. Quite amazingly modern tap fittings can lift the look of a place too. They bring about a very simple modernization of the kitchen and bathroom. Kitchens can often be upgraded quite cheaply with new bench tops and cupboard doors.

There are a number of fantastic products on the market now that allow you to paint areas that you could never paint before: tiles in the kitchen and bathroom, plastic and even glass.

Doing a remodeling job

This property investment strategy may be one for you or it may not. You could currently be in a situation where you are managing your loan repayments and everything is under control but you feel you want to keep improving your property portfolio but do not have enough deposit to purchase another.

An option available to you is to spend $25,000-$30,000 on a property upgrading and modernizing it. (Possibly a lot more if it is a big property.) You will then be able to increase your rent substantially. You may be a little negatively geared for a while, but then again you may not if the property is in an area where high rents are achievable. If you have added rooms the increase in the rent could be quite substantial.

What you have done is increase the value of your property and if the remodeling has been done correctly you could possibly have increased the property value by as much as $45,000-$50,000..

Taking this step the following will or could happen:

1. You have increased the attractiveness of the property and you should be able to receive a substantially increased rental at the property; and

2. With the proof of increased income from the property you can often get that extra loan you were looking for.

One point to remember is that if you are going to remodel a home and to get a high rent, the property does need to be located in an area where high rents are achievable. There is no point in doing an expensive remodeling job on a property that is in a low economic environment where renters just cannot afford high rents.

Doing capital improvements on a property are tax deductible so check with your Quantity Surveyor as to a

Real Estate Investing

Depreciation Schedule and make sure you get the full benefit of the improvement.

Taking all of this into account you may end up with a positive cash flow real estate with the increased rents.

FINANCE

There are several ways to finance real estate investments and the new investor will most likely be looking to finance through a finance company. Another alternative to finance company lending is to do private lending and we will touch on that in this chapter although it is not new investors usually do.

Fixed interest

A fixed interest loan is when you have a loan that is lent to you at a fixed interest rate. That means that you will be paying the agreed interest for the full term that the 'fixed interest' loan is for.

It could be that you have a fixed interest loan for 5 years and then revert to a variable loan or it could be fixed with a re-negotiation to take place at the end of the 5 years.

The downside of a fixed loan is that if the interest rates go down you do not get the benefit of it, but by the same token if the interest rates go up you are not put in a situation that you cannot afford given the same circumstances.

Variable (Adjustable) interest

With a variable loan you have agreed to pay the interest that is set by the finance company depending on its monetary policy at any given time throughout the term of the loan. This means that the interest will go up and down as the interest rates vary throughout the period of the loan.

This will work for you if the interest rates go down, but against you if the interest rates go up.

Interest only

An interest only loan means that for a set period you are going to be paying interest only on loan monies and no capital reduction with your repayments. These loans are not usually set up for a long period of time and are ones that usually come up for review after 2 or 3 years. The interest on these loans could be variable or fixed.

Some investors will take out this type of loan for the first couple of years to keep their repayments low and help with cash flow until they start getting rental increases.

Caution: A point to be aware of with an interest only loan is that you are not reducing your principal in any way, so should the property market prices devalue you could be left in a vulnerable position with less equity in the property than when the loan was first set up and the lending company may require a large principal payment or it could force a 'mortgagee sale'.

Interest and principal

An interest and principal loan means that you pay off interest and principal each time that you are making repayments. This in effect pays off the capital on the loan as well as the interest charge. Because of this the loan repayments work out to be higher than an interest only loan. In most cases it means that there is less principal being paid off in the earlier years as the interest is on the full value of the loan therefore higher initially, with more principal being paid off in the latter years as the principal value decreases over time and the interest component of the repayment is lower.

An interest and principal loan can be either fixed interest or variable interest.

Split loan

A split loan means that the total loan has been split between two or more methods of borrowing money, for example, an interest only fixed loan and a variable (adjustable) interest and principal loan. This can be a good way to go as you get the benefit of the interests rates going up and down and also there is the safety of some of the loan on a fixed repayment so that you do have a reasonable knowledge of what you have to pay each time.

There are various options with a split loan so you do need to discuss that with your mortgage broker.

New investors, or investors who are working to a tight budget, often like a loan with some fixed interest and some variable as this type of split loan gives them the advantage of both interest charges.

Private financing

Private financing is when a private person lends money to another (investor) with intention that interest is paid on the loan. Access to funds like this are usually through a solicitor or accountant but there are other sources as well.

Many private investors are people who do not want to be involved in personally purchasing real estate, but just want to get a good return on their investment.

To obtain private lending you do need to have a business plan written up and in quite some detail, so that the lender feels confident that you know what you are about. It also pays to have a resume attached to it so that they can see what you have been doing with your life.

Refinancing

Property investors, especially those with several properties should keep in touch with the finance market to see if they should be re-organizing their finances.

There are several reasons why you might look to refinance with the main ones being:

- Buying or selling properties – in other words a change in your asset base
  - Increasing or decreasing property prices
  - Increasing or decreasing interest rates
  - Change in personal income circumstances

Caution: Always check what your exit fees are before finalizing any refinance arrangements.

Increasing or decreasing property prices

If real estate prices are increasing you may want to take advantage of the additional equity in your real estate assets and purchase more properties. This may be the time for a refinancing situation to take place.

If property prices have decreased it means the equity you have in property has diminished and this is most definitely a time to look at your finances. Your finance company will want to make sure that there is enough equity for them should you default on your repayments so you may need to make sure of this by refinancing to reduce your monthly repayments, selling or taking on a personal loan (to pay down your loan) to cover the depressed period. Look at your options very carefully and act promptly should this situation arise.

Increasing or decreasing interest rates

Should interest rates change this will affect those on a variable interest loan. Those on fixed interest loans will stay the same.

A small change probably won't be worth worrying about but should interest rates change dramatically it could be time to refinance to take advantage of this change, especially if they go down. You may wish to change from a fixed interest to a variable interest.

Is there a pain factor? Sure there is!

If interest rates go down and you want to change to a variable rate you could be charged a large exit fee to get out of your loan. When the banks lent you the money they have borrowed it at a certain rate so they can lend it to you at a certain rate, so if you want to get out of that loan they expect to repay the initial loan at the cost that it was lent to them at the higher interest rate.

Whenever you consider refinancing do your sums very carefully and always find out all your costs to get out of your loan and your expenses to take out another loan.

When the global crisis hit and interest rates went down investors thought 'great, now I can refinance and get a better loan' but it did not quite happen like that. Rates had dropped several per cent but when people tried to refinance to take advantage of the lower interest rates they were asked to pay substantial sums to change existing loans. Many did not bother in the end as the cost of changing was too high.

When a lot of sellers had to sell and exit loans early, they were left with nothing in their hand after the sale because with the reduced real estate price and the exit fees on the loans there was nothing left for them to receive. In fact some still ended up with a large loan despite the fact they did not own real estate any more as there was still a difference between what the property sold for and the total of the loan payout.

Change in personal income circumstances

A change in personal income can be a factor for refinancing as well. For example, it could be a situation where a mum, who has taken several years off to look after children, now has a full-time job or the fact that someone has lost a job, or wants to cut back hours.

Any dramatic change in financial circumstances warrants a good look at your mortgage finances and again, do it sooner rather than later.

If for example one person was going to cut their hours back, it would be better to refinance while both are still employed because lenders are always wary when there has been a change in finances or a change in job and then the request is made.

PROPERTY MANAGEMENT

Property management is a very important part of making money with your property investment portfolio. There are several areas that need attention with property management.

Tenants

This of course is the first one that springs to mind. Unsuitable tenants could be tenants that just can't afford the rent, even though they look after the property but due to unforeseen circumstances such as illness or accident cannot pay the rent that they initially signed up to pay. Or they could be tenants that pay the rent, but mistreat the property along the way. Then the other scenario is where you have the ultimate bad tenant that doesn't pay or look after the property.

There are many more good tenants than there are bad tenants. I have heard an argument for the fact that it is better to buy good properties because you will attract a better tenant. This could work because higher rents are generally paid by people who have employment and these people tend to be better tenants, but it is not always the case.

Another group of tenants who are attractive to the landlord is the retiree. If they can afford your rent then these people can be the ideal tenant for several reasons:

- They want to stay long term
- They like to live in nice, but small homes so as a landlord you can purchase smaller and cheaper homes
- They look after the place because they have time on their hands

- Often they are receiving a 'living allowance' or rental assistance from the government
- They don't hold parties or do other outrageous things that damage the property

Rental increases

Charging a fair rent is something that should be considered at all times. I mean a fair rent for the landlord and for the tenant. Keeping good tenants can save the landlord a lot of money in the long run in vacancies, repairs and ongoing costs. A fair rent is one that suits both parties. If a property is let at a high rent it is probable that the tenants won't stay and even a one week vacancy in between rentals will mean that the extra rent that was sought initially could cost more in the long run than charging a reasonable rent in the first place and the tenant staying on at the property.

If you do have the 'perfect' tenant it pays to look after them. You may not put the rent up or you may pick up the garden maintenance when the next rent increase is due or do something to show your appreciation.

Not much different than being in a business where you need to look after good clients.

Repairs and maintenance

Overdue repairs could arise from the fact that few inspections of the property are carried out and little communication between parties is taking place. If maintenance is not carried out on a regular basis repairs can turn into major costs: things like bad electrical wiring, broken power sockets, leaking water pipes, mould in the walls, termites, etc. All these types of maintenance issues can turn into very expensive repairs if they are not caught in the very early stages with property inspections.

Self Managed Property

There are guidelines as to the rights of tenants and landlords and if a landlord is going to manage their own property it is imperative that they know the local residential tenancy laws and follow them. If a landlord does their own renting and does not know the local tenancy laws they leave themselves open to law suits and other problems with the law, especially if they have problem tenants.

Careful management of properties needs to take place to get the best financial benefit from owning investment properties.

Agreement for Property Management with a company

This method of management has many advantages which often outweigh the costs associated with having someone manage your property. There are certain legalities that need to be adhered to when managing a property and the management companies have trained staff to deal with these situations.

Having your property managed also allows you the freedom to get on with your life if you are working or if you want an active retirement lifestyle. For other landlords though, they are running their property investment portfolio as 'their business' and do want to be involved and are prepared to learn the required laws and systems to manage their properties correctly.

If you appoint a Property Management company make sure they adhere to what they say they will do for you. I have heard investors complain about the property management team they have employed regarding issues over a period of time, but the reality is that the investor does need to make sure and check that everything is in order regarding the property. Just like anything else, there are good property managers and not so good property managers, so if they say they are going to give you a written report every 3 months and they don't, then get on to it and rev them up. You are paying them, so make sure they are doing their job, if not, fire them.

You need to get reports on a regular basis because you don't want the property to fall into disrepair. Also make sure that property managers are going to let you know the minute a tenant is getting behind in payment. There could be genuine reasons for it which will resolve themselves, but if it becomes and issue you want to be on to it straight away.

Communication is the key.

BUSINESS PLAN

You might wonder why you would bother with a business plan and if this is the case you are also probably thinking that owning one or two investment properties is all you want to worry about.

Have you considered owning a substantial property investment portfolio?

The majority of investors stop at owning 2 or 3 investment properties and to be honest I don't know why, but my assumption is that they feel they have done well (and they have) and that when the time comes they can sell a property and live off the capital, and this is possible. But do you realize that this option will still only allow you a mediocre lifestyle, whereas if you kept building a property investment portfolio you could live a life of luxury if you wished.

If you have the ability either mentally and/or financially to buy 2 or 3 investment properties, I would have to ask, "why stop there when by owning 15 – 20 investment properties in a few years time, you could live a very comfortable and exciting retirement?"

You see you have obviously managed to get ahead and buy a couple of properties, but if you fine tune your steps and put them into a Business Plan you will be able to expand your portfolio.

The advantages of doing this are:
- Less risk of ending up with nothing financially if you manage your loans and repayments
- The chance to become very wealthy
- The chance to retire early and live off your property portfolio income
- The chance to stop your everyday employment and grow your investment portfolio at a great rate

The point is that if you have these goals in mind, a Business Plan would need to be written so that you have strict guidelines as to how to build the portfolio.

Here are some suggestions for you to put into your Property Investment Business Plan:

- Your goals – short term, medium term and long term
- What type of property you want to purchase, right down to the number of bedrooms, bathrooms, garages, location, age, construction, etc.
- Financial data – so that you are always ready to present what you have to your mortgage financier when you are seeking finance to purchase and so that you know roughly what your equity is at any given time so that you can make decisions to sell or buy as needed without too much delay
- Your buying strategy

- Your selling strategy
- Your risk strategy
- Education
- Your Team – contact details for all the people you use during your purchasing and selling process

You can see that by having a detailed plan you will more easily be able to grow your portfolio. It can seem to be time consuming and a bit of a pain in the neck to go through this process, but any system that makes money needs to have a detailed Plan of some sort otherwise managing it would just be a 'fly by the seat of your pants' operation.

If a commitment is made to make serious money from an investment portfolio it can be done, in fact is being done and many investors are finding that they are leading the lifestyle they had never dreamed of, purely and simply because they put the time into taking the steps necessary to become a professional property investor.

It is not rocket science but it does need commitment, education, planned steps, risk management and careful financial control to achieve the goals.

Real Estate Investing

The point is I am sure you have heard the old saying: "If you don't plan, you plan to fail." And that is surely what will happen if you do not have a plan for your real estate investment.

There are so many different aspects to consider and you need to break them down into 'must haves' so that you are not changing your mind every time you look at a new property.

When you seriously start looking at real estate to purchase then you need to have clear defined goals as to what you will look at.

Building Your Team Of Experts

When real estate investing, there are a number of different areas that need professional advice and it pays to build up a team to help you in this respect as they will be fluent with your goals and aspirations.

These are a list of services you need to foster and list in your Business Plan:

- Legal advisors
- Specialist Property Investing Accountant
- Mortgage lending contacts
- Quantity Surveyor
- A team of real estate contacts who have local knowledge who communicate well (one of the most complained about problems dealing with agents)
- Property management and inspection team
- Maintenance team

The point is that before you start purchasing property it is a good idea to build your team of experts so that when you get to the purchasing situation you can immediately get their advice.

One very relevant point to remember is to use professionals who are experienced in property investing. For example, you may have been a business owner for many years and have a good business accountant who is used to dealing with your type of business, but the reality is that accountants do specialize and if you are serious about making money from

Real Estate Investing

property investing you want an accountant who can advise you on all the tax benefits of decisions you have to make.

Selling Your Investment Real Estate

The practice of buying and holding real estate has changed somewhat over the past decade. There is a very strong school of thought that to hold a property for a long period of time is not the answer and to buy and sell is a better strategy.

This school of thought comes with the following ideas:

- If the property is in good condition and can be bought at a very good price, then buy and sell within a couple of years
- If the property can be bought at a good price but needs a little upgrading, then do that, hold if for several years and sell it on
- A property that needs serious remodeling can be bought, remodeled and sold on at any time after the remodeling is completed
- Buy properties that are in good locations and which are due for property increases due to various changes in the area. These changes could be industrial reasons, commercial reasons, major transport links or political reasons. Whatever the reason is, certain areas will attract price increases at certain times and these are worth following if this is a strategy that you want to follow – hold until the price levels out and then sell it on
- Expand your vision and look across country for properties and even internationally the more experienced you become

Selling when tenanted

When selling an investment property it is not a good idea to put in new tenants and straight away put the property on the market. There is a much better chance of co-operation from the tenants if they have had several months' enjoyment of the property before they are expected to have interruptions from listing agents. Tenants do have rights when the property is listed for sale and if you do have them onside then that is the better situation.

If you have tenants in the house with a lease and you sell the property to a home owner then check to see if in your area of location, the tenants have the right to stay in the home until the lease ends. Should this be the case and you sell to a home owner, the tenants are often happy to move if they are given a financial incentive. In other words they may happily move if you as the landlord agrees to pay the removal expenses and/or cleaning. This is just a way of negotiating a satisfactory settlement for everyone concerned.

Another step a landlord may take is to offer to have the grounds looked after during the sale period and that way you will know that the property has a tidy street appeal during the selling period. Or you may offer to have the house commercially cleaned prior to buyers starting to arrive and this could be a good incentive to get onside with the tenants too, as long as they don't take offense of course, so it would be imperative to have the importance of it all explained to them properly.

Check List For Purchasing Investment Property

Location
- Suburb
- Price Range
- House
- Townhouse
- Property aspect

Exterior of The Home
- Block Size
- Front Yard – Rear Yard
- Landscaping – Condition
- Mature Trees
- Home Appearance from Street
- Type of Home (Two Story, Single)
- Siding (Brick, Brick Veneer, Wood)
- Condition of House and Paint
- Attached or Detached Garage
- One, Two Three Car Garage
- Condition of Walkways
- Covered Front Porch
- Enclosed Front Porch
- Fenced Backyard
- Privacy
- Patio-Decking
- Swimming Pool
- Storage Shed
- Type of Roof – General Condition

- Type of Foundation
- Structural Appearance
- Possible Problems

Interior of The Home
- Separate Front Hallway
- Soundproofing

Doors and Windows
- Types of Windows
- Open and Close Window without Sticking
- General Condition
- Locks and latches work

Kitchen
- General Size and Colors
- Eat-In Area
- Sufficient Cupboard Space
- Pantry
- Single or Double Sink-Condition
- Sufficient Counter Top Area
- Floor Type-Condition

Other Rooms – Features
- Number and size of Bedrooms
- Number of Bathrooms
- Fireplace Type
- Signs of Moisture
- Cracks in Walls and Floors

Recent Renovations
- Done By Seller or Professional Renovator

Systems Electrical: Plumbing
Water service
Sewer or septic system
Heating type
Air conditioning
Hot water heater
Insulation type
Ask to see copies of recent utility bills
Cable or aerial TV service: adequate room outlets
Internet access: high speed; dial up
Other notable features and comments
Community – Close To:
- Shops
- Public Transport
- Medical Facilities (Hospitals, Doctors, Dentists)
- Local Clubs
- Parks
- Golf Course
- Public Swimming Pools

Public Tennis Courts

Restaurants

Theatres

Public Library

Major Roads and Highways

Local Neighborhood

- Urban, Suburban, Rural
- Older or Newer; Estimated Age
- Types of Homes In Area
- Age Group of Area Homeowners
- Quiet Streets
- Adequate Streetlights
- Visible Power Lines and Telephone Poles
- Well Maintained Homes
- Sidewalks
- Space between Homes
- Adequate Street Parking

To Print Off This Checklist Go To My Author Site And Download the PDF file:

http://kayedennanauthor.com/real-estate-purchasing-checklist/

Take care with your projects and decisions, research and verify information you receive. Keep educating yourself as strategies and rules and regulations are constantly changing.

About The Author

Kaye Dennan was a real estate principal for 5 years and has spent the last 5 years as a blog writer for real estate investing sites. Kaye has an extensive knowledge on real estate investing due to being and investor for many years and has written this book in order to help readers who would like to start real estate investing.

Given that the book can be bought worldwide some facts may not be applicable to your area. Regardless of that though, because real estate laws change on a constant basis, do check all facts and figures before you make a commitment.

From the Author

I have written a number of ebooks and books pertaining to home based businesses and lifestyle topics. If you would like to visit my author page on Amazon you will see the full range:

http://www.amazon.com/-/e/B00AVQ6KKM

www.ingramcontent.com/pod-product-compliance
Lightning Source LLC
Chambersburg PA
CBHW071646170526
45166CB00003B/1447